The Robot Book

Rebecca Silverstein

Brought to you by the editors of

My Weekly Reader

Children's Press®
An imprint of Scholastic Inc.

How to Read This Book

This book is for kids and grown-ups to read together—side by side!

A 😊 means it is the kid's turn to read.

A grown-up can read the rest.

Simple text for kids who are learning to read

Harder text—which builds knowledge and vocabulary— for grown-ups to read aloud

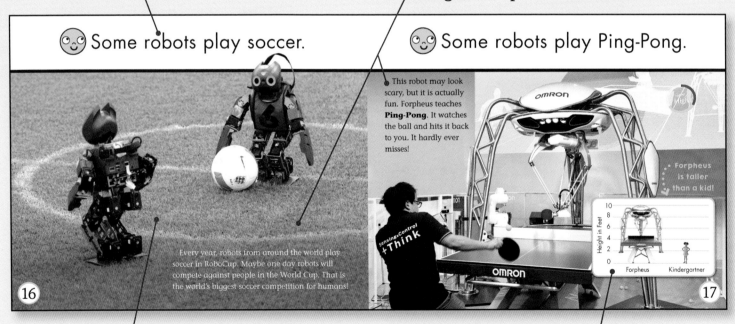

😊 Some robots play soccer.

Every year, robots from around the world play soccer in RoboCup. Maybe one day robots will compete against people in the World Cup. That is the world's biggest soccer competition for humans!

16

😊 Some robots play Ping-Pong.

This robot may look scary, but it is actually fun. Forpheus teaches **Ping-Pong**. It watches the ball and hits it back to you. It hardly ever misses!

Forpheus is taller than a kid!

Height in Feet
10
8
6
4
2
0
Forpheus   Kindergartner

17

Bright photos to talk about

Nonfiction text features like graphs and captions

Table of Contents

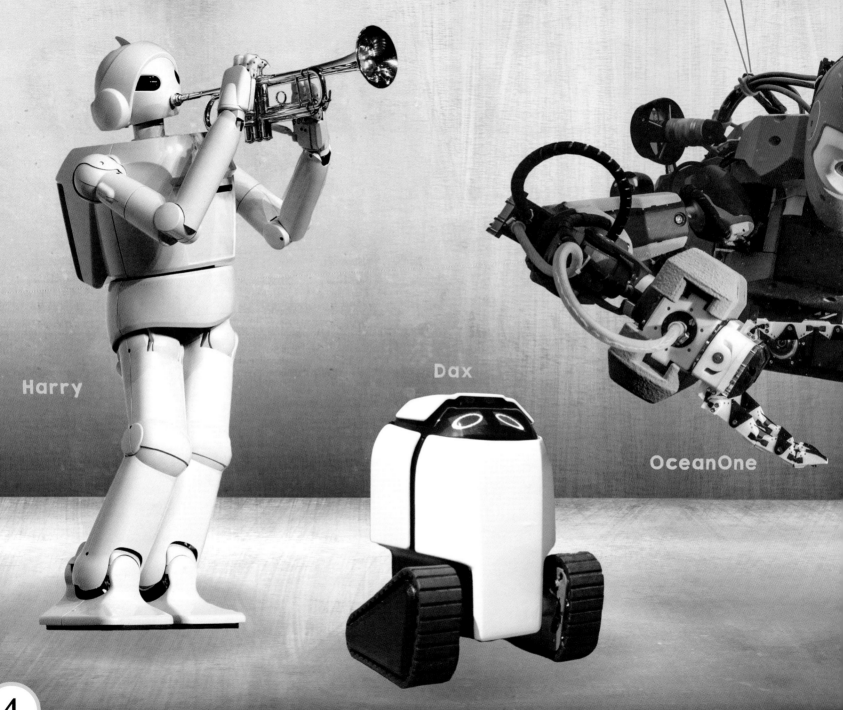

Harry

Dax

OceanOne

4

Chapter I

Robots to the Rescue

Why do people make robots? To help out!

Robot chef

Nao

Robots can help us cook.

Robot **chefs** help in kitchens. They put sauce and toppings on pizzas. Then they place the pizzas into an oven. But humans have the best job. They eat the pizzas!

Robots can help us explore.

diver

OceanOne helps us explore the ocean. It can go deeper underwater than humans can. It can explore shipwrecks on the ocean floor! Scientists control OceanOne using a **joystick**.

Robots can help us shop.

This robot helps neighborhood stores make deliveries. First, shopkeepers put items in Dax's "belly." Then Dax rolls to your house. Ding-dong! Dax is at the door!

Fun fact: Dax's first delivery was a burrito!

Dax's belly

Chapter 2

Animal Robots

Animals can run, swim, and climb. So can some animal robots!

This robot moves like a cheetah.

This robot moves like a gecko.

What is climbing up the window? It is Stickybot! It climbs like a gecko. Tiny hairs on a gecko's toes stick to walls. **Engineers** gave Stickybot rubber hairs on its toes.

The tiny hairs on a gecko's feet are called setae.

This robot moves like a bee.

Buzz! RoboBee is a tiny **drone**.
A drone is a robot that flies without a pilot.
RoboBee flies like a bee. It also swims in water!

RoboBee

real bee

This robot moves like a kangaroo.

Can you hop like a kangaroo? This robot can! BionicKangaroo has springy legs like a real kangaroo. The only thing that's missing is a pouch to carry a **joey**.

A kangaroo can jump the length of two cars!

This robot moves like a fish.

A robot called SoFi moves just like a real fish. Its floppy back **fin** lets it wiggle through water. SoFi looks so real that fish don't even notice it swimming past.

This robot moves like a snake.

This robot snake is called Uncle Sam. It **slithers** like a snake. It can wrap its body around a tree and wriggle up the trunk. Best of all, it never bites!

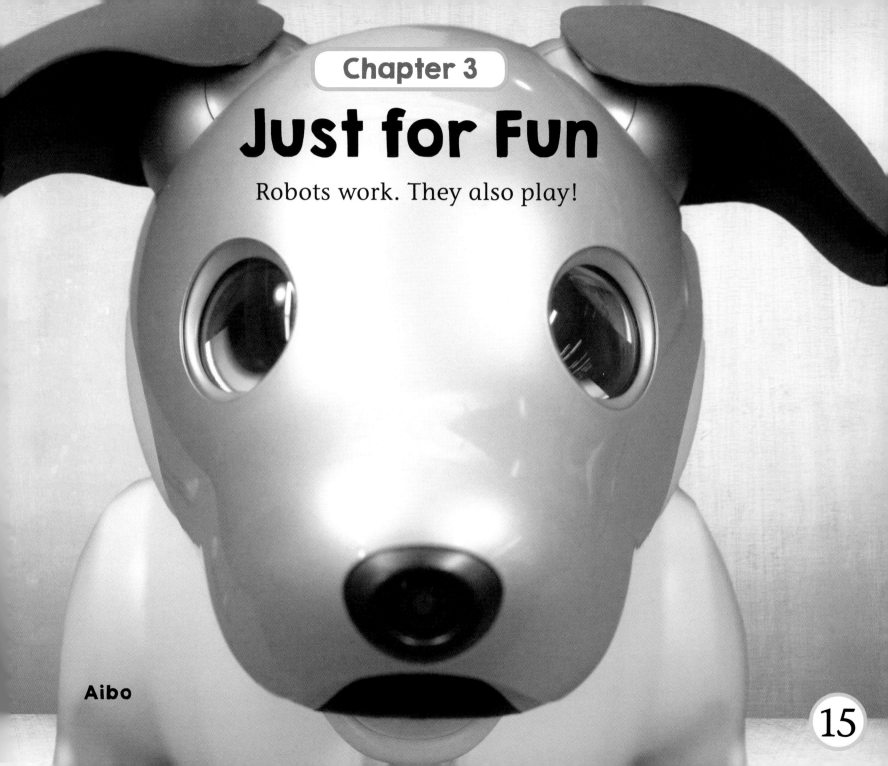

Chapter 3

Just for Fun

Robots work. They also play!

Aibo

Some robots play soccer.

Every year, robots from around the world play soccer in RoboCup. Maybe one day robots will compete against people in the World Cup. That is the world's biggest soccer competition for humans.

Some robots play Ping-Pong.

This robot may look scary, but it is actually fun. Forpheus teaches **Ping-Pong**. It watches the ball and hits it back to you. It hardly ever misses!

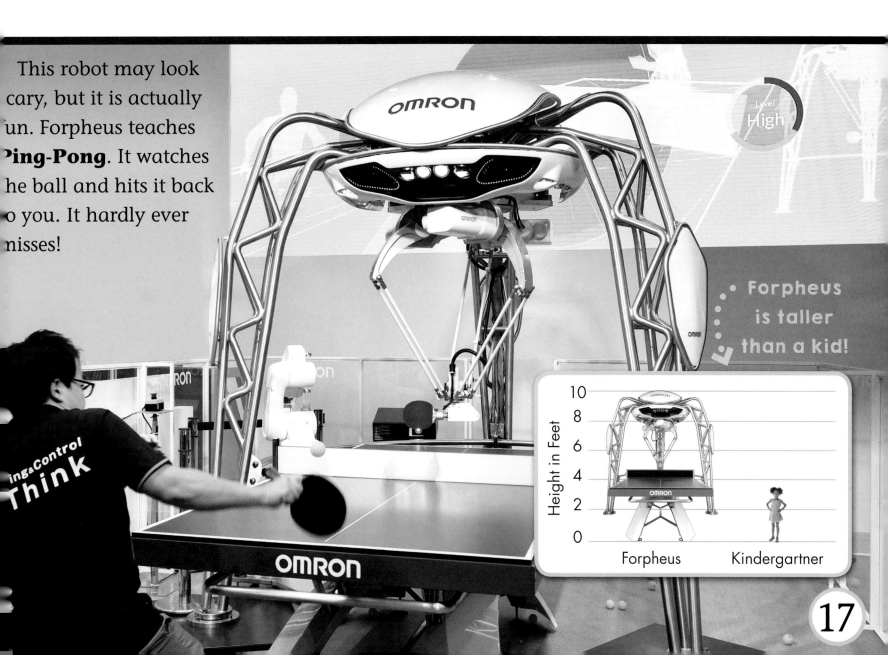

Level
High

Forpheus
is taller
than a kid!

Height in Feet

10
8
6
4
2
0

Forpheus   Kindergartner

Some robots play music.

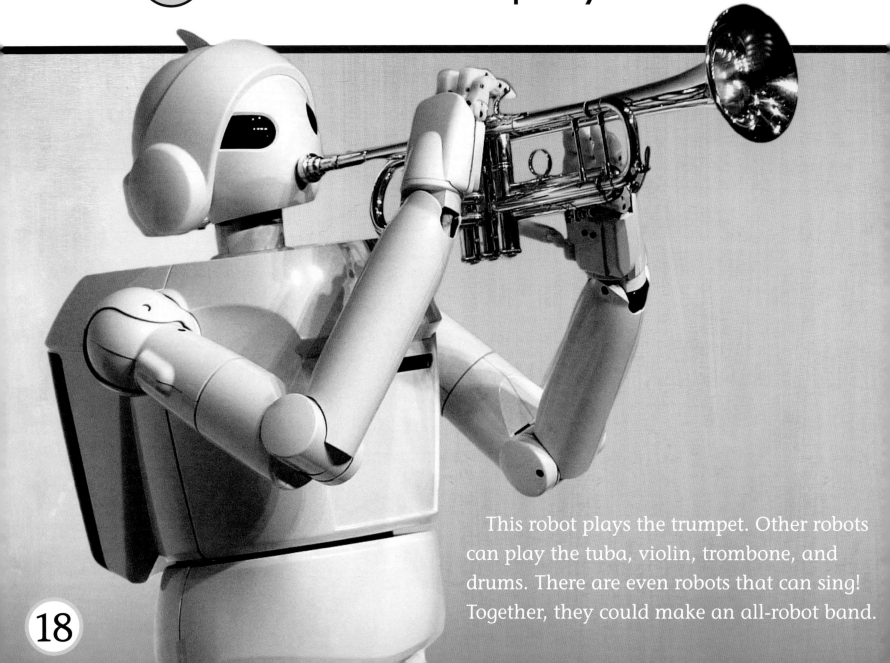

This robot plays the trumpet. Other robots can play the tuba, violin, trombone, and drums. There are even robots that can sing! Together, they could make an all-robot band.

☺ Some robots dance.

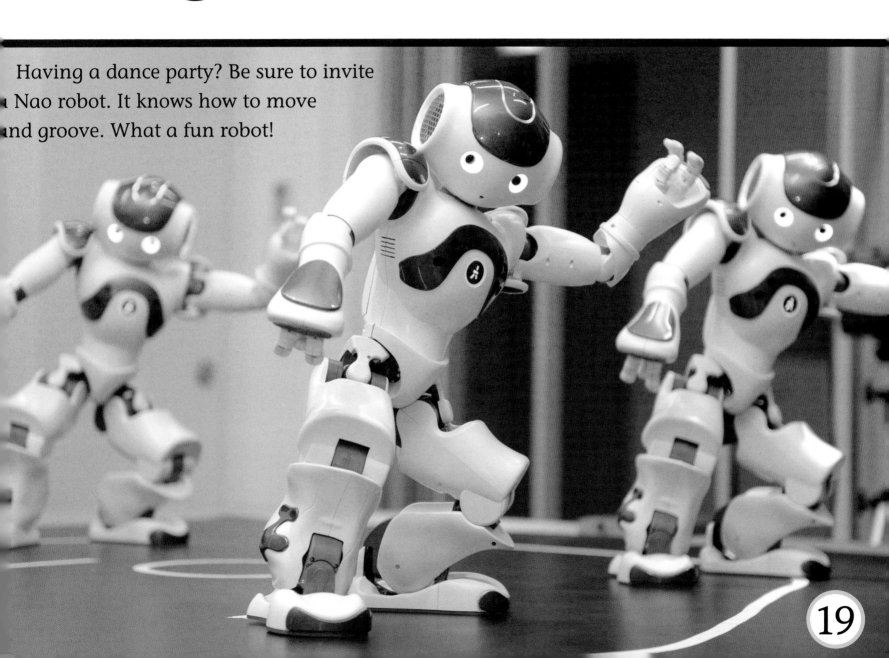

Having a dance party? Be sure to invite a Nao robot. It knows how to move and groove. What a fun robot!

Some robots are pets.

Your next pet could be a robot! Aibo is a playful robot puppy that acts like a real dog. It can do tricks, like kicking a ball. Woof, woof!

Do you want a pet robot?

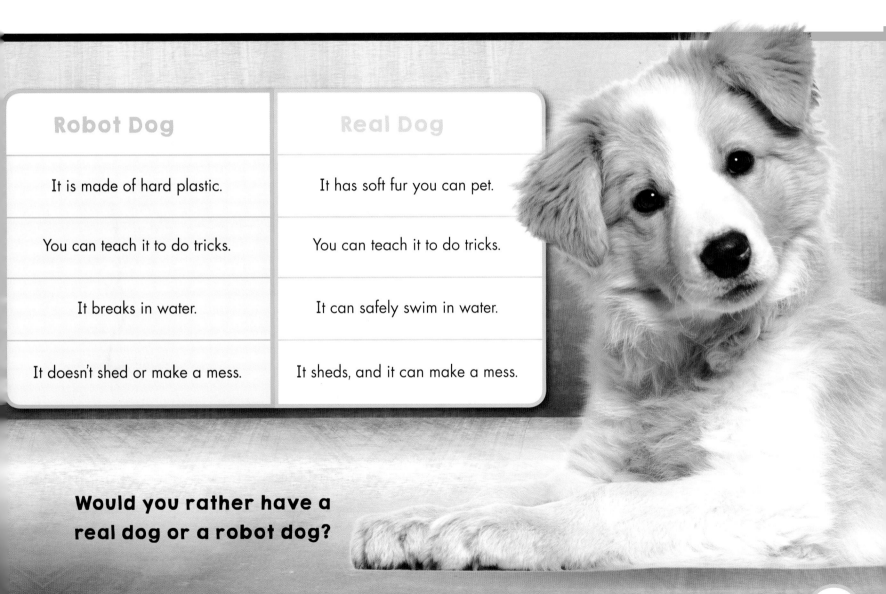

Robot Dog	Real Dog
It is made of hard plastic.	It has soft fur you can pet.
You can teach it to do tricks.	You can teach it to do tricks.
It breaks in water.	It can safely swim in water.
It doesn't shed or make a mess.	It sheds, and it can make a mess.

Would you rather have a real dog or a robot dog?

Glossary

chefs: (shefs)
People who
cook food as a job

engineers: (en-juh-**nirz**)
People who build robots
and other machines

drone:
(drohn) A robot
that flies without
a pilot

fin: (fin)
The part of a
fish that helps it
steer or move

joey:
(joh-ee):

A baby kangaroo

joystick:
(joi-stik)

A kind of remote that controls robots, cars, planes, and games

Ping-Pong: **(ping**-pong)

A game where you hit a ball over a net on a table. It is also called table tennis.

slithers: **(slih**-therz)

Moves by twisting and sliding, like a snake

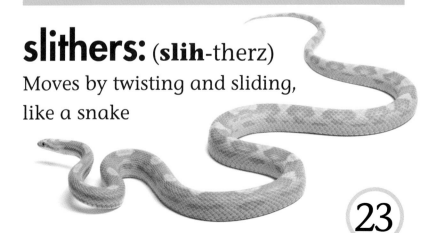

23

Index

Photos ©: cover main: Barry Chin/The Boston Globe/Getty Images; cover face icons and throughout: Giuseppe_R/Shutterstock; back cover: Courtesy of Mark Cutkosky/Stanford University; 3: BSIP/UIG/Getty Images; 4 background and throughout: Eky Studio/Shutterstock; 4 left: Kurita Kaku/Gamma-Rapho/Getty Images; 4 center bottom: Natalie Behring/Getty Images; 4 right: Osada/Seguin/DRASSM; 5 bottom left: Barry Chin/The Boston Globe/Getty Images; 5 bottom center: stockcreations/Shutterstock; 5 right: Ingo Wagner/AFP/Getty Images; 6: Ingo Wagner/AFP/Getty Images; 7: Osada/Seguin/DRASSM; 8 main: Natalie Behring/Getty Images; 8 inset: bonchan/Shutterstock; 9: José-Luis Olivares/MIT; 10 left: Courtesy of Mark Cutkosky/Stanford University; 10 right: Walter Rohdich/Minden Pictures; 11 right honeybee: Tsekhmister/Shutterstock; 11 background: Vector8DIY/Shutterstock; 11 left RoboBee: Wyss Institute/Harvard University; 12 background: dwph/Shutterstock; 12 inset: Tobias Titz/Getty Images; 12 right: Festo AG & Co. KG.; 13 main: Joseph DelPreto/MIT; 13 inset: ChiccoDodiFC/iStockphoto; 14 main: Biorobotics Lab/Carnegie Mellon University; 14 inset: Stephen Clarke/Shutterstock; 15: The Asahi Shimbun/Getty Images; 16: VCG/Getty Images; 17 inset right: Africa Studio/Shutterstock; 17 main: Kazuhiro Nogi/AFP/Getty Images; 17 inset left: CB2/ZOB/Supplied by WENN/Newscom; 18: Kurita Kaku/Gamma-Rapho/Getty Images; 19: Yoshikazu Tsuno/AFP/Getty Images; 20 dog: The Yomiuri Shimbun/AP Images; 20 ball: Kyodo News/Getty Images; 21: Eric Isselee/Shutterstock; 22 top left: Africa Studio/Shutterstock; 22 top right: science photo/Shutterstock; 22 bottom left: Wayne Hutchinson/Alamy Images; 22 bottom right: Eric Isselee/Shutterstock; 23 top left: Anan Kaewkhammul/Shutterstock; 23 top right: FangXiaNuo/iStockphoto; 23 bottom left: Emanuele Ravecca/Shutterstock; 23 bottom right: Eric Isselee/Shutterstock.

Library of Congress Cataloging-in-Publication Data

Names: Silverstein, Rebecca, author.
Title: The robot book / by Rebecca Silverstein.
Description: New York, NY: Children's Press®, an imprint of Scholastic Inc.,
[2019] | Series: Side by side | Includes index.
Identifiers: LCCN 2019004850| ISBN 9780531238400 (library binding) |
ISBN 9780531246573 (pbk.)
Subjects: LCSH: Robots--Juvenile literature.
Classification: LCC TJ211.2 .S5445 2019 | DDC 629.8/92--dc23

Brought to you by the editors of *Let's Find Out*®. Original Design by Whitney Highfield, Joan Michael and Judith E. Christ for Scholastic Inc.

2 3 4 5 6 7 8 9 10 R 29 28 27 26 25 24 23 22 21 20